Bella's Vietnam Adventure

Written By Stacey Zolt Hara

Illustrated By Steve Pileggi

"To Bryan, who first imagined the story of this charmed life." – SZH

For information, address Travel with Bella via email at info@travelwithbella.com.
www.travelwithbella.com

Composed in Singapore
Illustrated in the United States of America
Printed in Malaysia
First impression 2011
ISBN: 978-981-08-9882-3

"I've never seen so many bikes before," I tell Mommy as we stand on a busy corner, trying to cross the street in Hanoi.

Hanoi is one of the biggest cities in Vietnam, but there are very few cars here - just lots and lots of motorbikes. When we take a taxi in Chicago, where I was born, the driver won't take more than four of us, but these motorbikes fit a mommy, a daddy, a kid and sometimes a baby too.

The bikes whiz by us. There are no traffic lights. No blinking green man telling us it's safe to walk across the street. My mom and dad look at each other and take a deep breath. They may not win the family safety award today, but they will get us across this street.

"OK Bella, Daddy is going to carry you, and when we see a break in the traffic we're gonna make a run for it," Mom says.

"But Mama, at my school in Singapore, Teacher Alice says we always have to cross only at the crosswalk, wait for a green man, and then look both ways to make sure no cars are coming. Only then can we cross the street."

"Bella, this isn't Singapore, and it's not Chicago. Vietnam doesn't have all the things that make life so simple and easy. There's no green man to guide us. We just need to use our instincts and be smart, otherwise we will have to spend the entire day on this corner," Mom says.

"C'mon Bella, it's all part of the adventure," Dad says.

So I jump into Daddy's arms, ready to go, but we stand there waiting and waiting for the bikes to slow. My parents seem to have lost their courage.

Then, a Vietnamese man walks right past us, straight into traffic - the bikes seem to just pause for him to get by. How'd he **DO** that?

Daddy has a plan. We wait for the next Vietnamese person to approach the corner and we bravely cross along with him, following his lead and rhythm.

The bikes, cars and carts all slow as we approach, and people on the motorbikes are waving to me.

This is so much fun!

Giggling, I cheer when we reach the opposite side of the street.

"We did it! Nice work, Mom and Dad," I say, giving them High 5's. "Can we do it again?"

My mom and dad just look back at me, jaws open and faces pale, trying to catch their breath. Looking at each other, my parents say at the exact same time, "I don't think so."

Together, we walk along Hoan Kiem Lake. The bright red Sunbeam Bridge with its yellow Chinese characters crosses the lake, and a small pagoda crowns the center of the water.

People jog and ladies speed walk in pairs to get their morning exercise. Elderly men and young couples sit on tiny stools enjoying a snack or cuddling with a friend under a shady tree.

A young woman wears a blue flowered dress and a traditional triangular straw hat to shield the sun. Even with a large wooden stick balanced on her shoulder and a basket dangling off each end, she is as graceful as a ballerina.

One basket holds vegetables, the other side a big pot of soup called pho. It smells delicious.

The man crouches onto a small stool and enjoys his soup.

"Hey guys, when's lunch?" I ask my parents. "That smells yummy!"

After braving another street crossing, we tuck into one of the side streets around the the lake. Each street is organized like a section of a shopping mall. One street has all shoe shops, the next street sells only luggage, the next one mattresses, the next car parts, the next electronics.

You can buy everything here!

The number of shops is dizzying, as are the storekeepers working the sidewalks to lure us in. "We give good discount for you...Where you from?...Come buy from me, I sell nice things!"

I've never seen so many shoes before! Mommy and I can't resist.

On one shelf sit a pair of sparkly ruby red slippers, just like the ones Dorothy wears in the Wizard of Oz. Bargaining is a must when shopping in Hanoi, so Mommy tells me I can have them only if I can strike a deal.

"Excuse me, how much for these?" I ask the shopkeeper.

"$10, little girl. Where you from?" he asks.

"I'm from Chicago, but I live in Singapore. My name is Bella and I'm five years old."

"Well Bella, it's nice to meet you," he says, shaking my hand.
"Do you like these shoes?"

"Yes," I say, "but I will only spend $5."

"$5?!? Too cheap, ah. You pay $7," the shopkeeper says, driving a hard bargin.

"OK, $7. It's a deal," I say, as I shake his hand. He packs my shoes in a plastic bag, and I walk down the street, beaming with pride.

Mom and Dad don't want to brave the street crossing again, so we decide to take cyclos back to our hotel. In Hanoi, you can hail a cyclo the same way you would a taxi in a big city in America. The man on the bicycle pushes the cart while you sit in it.

Mommy and I take the yellow one, Daddy the blue one.

I hold my hand out to the driver. "Hi, my name is Isabelle, but you can call me Bella," I say. "Can you drive us to our hotel? We can't cross the street without the green man."

The driver smiles and lifts me onto the bench. I give him a High-5. "I'd like a really fast ride please."

"How 'bout just a safe ride?," Mommy says as she climbs in and hoists me onto her lap, using her arms around me as a seat belt.

Dad's cyclo pulls up next to us. My dad has his video camera in hand, ready to capture our adventure through the city.

Suddenly, Daddy's face lights up like a little boy about to get in trouble, "Hurry up girls - last one there is a rotten egg!"

We take off into the streets, the motor bikes whizzing around us.

From our cyclos we can see everything: ladies walking down the street with baskets of food balanced on their heads, buildings with delicate French-inspired balconies and Chinese-style pagodas on top, and women selling bananas from two baskets balanced on their shoulders like old-fashioned scales. The women in Vietnam are really strong.

A Vietnamese mommy and daughter on a motorbike slow to ride next to us, smiling and waving.

A couple surrounded by bolts of colorful fabric at their shop run out into the street when they see us pass, their faces beaming with delight.

When the cyclos pull in front of the hotel, I feel like a princess climbing out of her chariot. The bell man in his stately uniform with the gold tassels holds out his hand so I can climb down, then opens the fancy door for me to enter the chandelier-lit lobby.

The next morning, we fly to Danang, and drive into Hoi An, a small village on the coast of China Beach with narrow streets and hundreds of small Chinese-style shophouses, where traditional tailors whip up custom-made outfits in no time.

"A long, long time ago - even before Grandma and Grandpa were born - people from all over Asia used to come to Hoi An to trade with each other. That's why you see French, Chinese and Japanese touches in every building, and in the food we eat here," Mom tells me as we walk over the Japanese Covered Bridge.

"In the old days," Dad explains, "people would make their own things to sell, just like they did a long time ago in America. When your Great Great Grandparents came to America from Russia, they worked as tailors, making clothing custom fit for each customer.

Today the tailors in Hoi An do the same thing," Dad says. "How about we go to a shop and you can pick out your own fabric to make a dress?"

Inside the tailor shop, there was every fabric imaginable - scratchy wool, soft striped cotton, smooth silk with Chinese characters and satin in every color of the rainbow. Daddy wants to make shirts for work, so I help him by picking out some of my favorite colors and patterns, but he says purple and pink polka dots are not his style.

For my dress, I choose a red satin to match my new red ruby slippers. The seamstress measures my arms, legs, waist and neck with a long measuring tape.

When we come back a few hours later, I try on the dress - it's perfect!

Poofy short sleeves like a princess, with a sash to match. I feel so beautiful, and all the ladies in the shop take their picture with me as a souvenir of the American girl with the chubby cheeks and wild curly hair.

Back at our hotel, after a long day of touring and shopping, we take a walk on China Beach. The soft, white sand creeps between my toes as I run to Daddy. Mom giggles, taking pictures with the waves crashing behind us.

Daddy lifts me up over his head as Mommy hugs us both from behind. I whisper to them both, "Can we visit Vietnam every day?"

Bella's Vietnam Adventure Curriculum Guide

Help your kids or students learn more about Vietnam with these activities, designed to enhance the reading experience at home or in the classroom.

Vietnamese Hats

Making and decorating Vietnamese-style hats is an easy, fun way to teach kids about traditional culture and style. As you make the hats, talk about the cultivation of rice throughout Asia, explaining to the kids that these triangular hats are worn during rice harvesting to shield farmers from the sun.

Using a 8.5x11 or A4 size sheet of paper, place a bowl upside down and trace the circle onto the page. Let each child decorate the area in the circle with colorful markers or crayons.

Then, cut a 2 inch wide triangular slice out of one side of the circle, with the top point of the triangle at the center of the circle. Pull the ends of the cut out together so the hat takes its shape, secure with tape. Use an elastic string to create a chin strap, stapling or taping it on either end.

Tailor Made

The quaint UNESCO certified town of Hoi An is famous for its tailor shops, which can whip up a custom-made outfit in hours. In this activity, kids will learn about the job of a tailor by designing their own clothing.

You'll need an assortment of fabric scraps in a wide range of colors, patterns and textures. Print out one mannequin worksheet template for each child from the parent/teacher corner at www.travelwithbella.com.

Have the kids cut pictures from magazines of their favorite clothes for inspiration. Then have them sketch the outfit on the mannequin worksheet.

Using the fabric scraps, the kids can draw the clothing, cut it out and paste it on the mannequins. Each one will be a bespoke creation, just like Bella's red dress!

Fabulous Pho

Bella marvels at the yummy smell of pho in Hanoi. Here's a simplified recipe for kids to sample this local delicacy's scent and taste too.

4 quarts beef broth

6 slices ginger root

2 big handfuls of bean sprouts

1 cup fresh mint leaves

1 teaspoon whole black peppercorns

1/4 cup fish sauce

2 8 oz packages dried rice noodles

2 large onions, halved

1 pound sirloin, thinly sliced

1 cup fresh basil leaves

1 cinnamon stick

1 cup cilantro leaves

2 limes cut into wedges

1/3 teaspoon hoisin sauce

1. Make the soup first: combine the broth, onion, ginger, lemon grass, cinnamon and peppercorns in a large pot. Boil, then reduce heat to a simmer. Cover for one hour.

2. Set up your garnishes: There's lots of ways customize pho with garnishes. Lay out the sprouts, mint, basil, cilantro and limes on a platter and set the hoisin sauce on the side.

3. Noodles: Cook the noodles in hot (not boiling) water, in a covered pot, for 15 minutes or until soft. Drain, then put in individual serving bowls.

4. Soup's on: Ladle the soup into the bowls and lay the raw beef on top, stirring the broth to cook the beef.

5. Just the right taste: Pass the garnish platter, letting the kids toss in the ingredients to suit their taste buds, just like the man at Hoan Kiem Lake.

Enjoy!